FORTNITE BATTLE ROYALE HACKS

SECRETS OF THE ISLAND

THE UNOFFICAL GUIDE TO TIPS AND TRICKS THAT OTHER GUIDES WON'T TEACH YOU

JASON R. RICH

Sky Pony Press
New York

Sky Pony Press books may be purchased in bulk at special discounts for sales promotion, corporate gifts, fund-raising, or educational purposes. Special editions can also be created to specifications. For details, contact the Special Sales Department, Sky Pony Press, 307 West 36th Street, 11th Floor, New York, NY 10018 or info@skyhorsepublishing.com.

Sky Pony® is a registered trademark of Skyhorse Publishing, Inc.®, a Delaware corporation.

Visit our website at www.skyponypress.com.

Authors, books, and more at SkyPonyPressBlog.com.

10 9 8 7 6 5 4 3 2

Library of Congress Cataloging-in-Publication Data is available on file.

Cover design by Brian Peterson

Print ISBN: 978-1-5107-4188-1
E-Book ISBN: 978-1-5107-4189-8

Printed in the United States of America

TABLE OF CONTENTS

SECTION 1

DISCOVER WHAT'S NEW
ON THE ISLAND

The popularity of Epic Games's *Fortnite: Battle Royale* continues to grow throughout the world as gamers are able to face new and exciting challenges by taking on the role of a soldier who is dropped onto a mysterious island that's being ravaged by a deadly storm. It's a non-stop quest for survival, as each soldier must stay alive longer than the 99 others, and be the last person standing at the conclusion of each match. Thanks to the movement and expansion of the storm, each match lasts approximately 15 action-packed minutes.

Whether you're experiencing *Fortnite: Battle Royale* on a Windows PC, Mac, Xbox One, PlayStation 4, iPhone, iPad, or Android-based mobile device, the challenges you face will be the same, yet your experience will be totally different each time you step foot on the island. The actions of the other soldiers, as well as the movement of the storm, ultimately determine what survival strategies you'll need to implement.

Brace for impact.

Breaking news! On May 1, 2018, comets crashed into the island.

To keep the gameplay fresh, every two weeks or so Epic Games tweaks the game a bit by introducing new weapons, challenges, and loot. In addition, every few months, a new "season" of challenges is introduced, and with each new season come some dramatic gameplay twists.

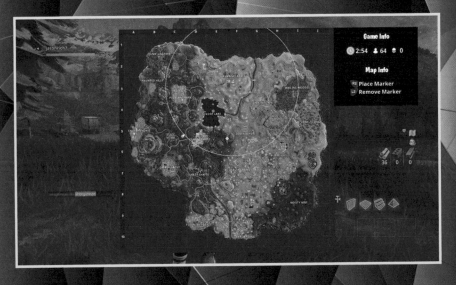

This is the island map from Season 3, prior to the crash-landing of the mysterious comets. Today, the map features several new places to explore—and it's constantly evolving.

When Season 4 kicked off in May 2018, players discovered that the area once known as Dusty Depot now contains a large crater. In the center of this crater is Dusty Divot—a futuristic research facility that contains all-new areas to explore.

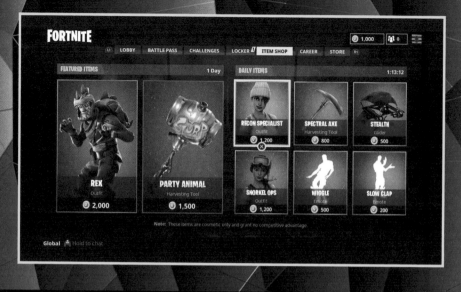

New daily challenges and Battle Passes are continuously introduced, and new character outfits, as well as Daily Items, can be purchased from the Item Shop (shown) or unlocked by making certain achievements within the game. Keep in mind, while you can fully customize the appearance of your character's outfit, back bling, pickaxe, and glider example, these visual enhancements have zero impact on your soldier's fighting abilities or strength.

The map on the previous page shows what the island map looked like for Season 4. A comet has utterly destroyed Dusty Depot (once found near section G5 of the map). This area is now known as Dusty Divot.

Because Dusty Divot offers an entirely new area to explore, it has become an extremely popular landing destination as soldiers depart the Battle Bus and skydive down to land. For this reason, the moment you land, it's essential that you locate and grab weapons and be prepared to fight! If you fail to grab a weapon, within seconds, your unarmed soldier will be shot by adversaries who landed sooner and knew exactly where to look to find their weapons.

If your desired landing destination is Dusty Divot, consider landing outside the crater instead of its middle. First, gather weapons, ammo, and resources (wood, stone, and metal), and then make your way onto the base. Dusty Divot will likely be crowded, so engaging in battles is inevitable. Remember, the goal of *Fortnite: Battle Royale* is to stay alive and be the last soldier standing. While you're rewarded for defeating adversaries, the more times you attack enemies or need to defend against their attacks, the more likely you are to be defeated.

There Are New Points of Interest to Explore

Located in a mountain near Snobby Shores (at least during Season 4) is a new supervillain base. A new mega-mansion is also located near Lonely Lodge. As you explore Salty Springs, be on the lookout for a new underground bunker that's filled with surprises.

Within Moisty Mire, you'll discover a new movie set area that's worth checking out. Another new location to explore is the remains of a dance club. Sections 2 and 6 of this guide focus on more of the new locations found on the island, as well as strategies for navigating around more familiar locations.

Seen on the previous page, Risky Reels is another new point of interest. It's an abandoned drive-in movie theater located near coordinates H2 on the island map. Here you'll discover a bunch of cars you can smash using your pickaxe to collect metal. There are also buildings chock-full of goodies that you should explore in this area.

Ways to Collect Weapons, Loot, and Ammo

The main focus of *Hacks for Fortnite: Battle Royale—Secrets of the Island* is to help you prepare for and win battles that take place anywhere on the island, avoid the deadly storm, and make it easier for you to safely explore different areas of the island.

On the island map, there are 20 labeled areas. These are known as **points of interest**. Each point of interest, whether it's Shifty Shafts, Lucky Landing, Retail Row, or Wailing Woods, offers different types of terrain to explore, as well as different obstacles to encounter.

As you can see on the previous page, each point of interest (and its surrounding areas) contains a selection of loot and weapons. Some loot and weapons will be easily visible—often lying on the ground, out in the open. As you're exploring, simply grab these items, as long as there's space in your backpack.

Other loot, weapons, and ammo will be hidden in the attics, main rooms, or basements of buildings. You should also look carefully below staircases or behind furniture. Use your pickaxe to smash furniture, collect wood, and see what's behind it.

Each point of interest also contains growing chests, like the one seen on the previous page. Each chest includes a random selection of loot, weapons, and ammo. While the contents of these chests changes, their locations typically remain the same. When you discover a chest, remember its location, so you can quickly locate it during future matches. Some chests eventually respawn, so if you're not the first soldier to discover any of them, you still may get the chance to find a filled chest.

Periodically, hot-air balloons carrying chests of loot randomly fall from the sky. These are **Supply Drops**. They typically offer a nice selection of weapons, ammo, and loot. When you notice one of these, approach with extreme caution. One or more of your adversaries may be lurking nearby, waiting to launch a surprise ambush as you approach. If you successfully reach the landing area of a Supply Drop, quickly build a series of walls around it and yourself using the resources you've collected.

Vending Machines can be found within many points of interest. When you approach one of these machines, you'll be able to purchase weapons and items using resources (wood, stone, or metal). When you approach a Vending Machine, you may be vulnerable to an attack, so build walls around yourself for protection.

The moment a soldier is defeated, all of their loot, weapons, ammo, loot, and resources drop to the ground and can be collected by anyone nearby. This is yet another way to build up your arsenal with powerful weapons and ammo, as well as useful loot.

Ammo boxes can be found throughout the island. These are non-descript boxes that do not glow. When you open them, you'll receive additional ammo that can be used in conjunction with your more powerful weapons.

Manage the Contents of Your Backpack

Your soldier's backpack can hold up to six different weapons and items (including your pickaxe). In some cases, you can hold several of the same item in one backpack slot. This applies to items like Bandages, Med Kits, and other types of loot that will be explained shortly. The contents of your backpack is continuously displayed on the screen. The location will vary based on which gaming system you're using.

A good selection of weapons to find and carry with you during a match includes an assault rifle, a shotgun, and a sniper rifle. Depending on what's happening is the match, round out your arsenal (and fill the last spots in your backpack) with other weapons or tools as needed. For example, a pistol is ideal for close-range combat.

While your pickaxe is always positioned in the leftmost slot of your backpack, once the other slots are filled, you have the ability to switch around slot positions, making it faster to scroll through and access what you will use most often. This is done from the Backpack Inventory screen, which is accessible during a match.

Once your backpack fills up, it'll often become necessary to drop items you no longer want or need to make room for more powerful and useful weapons and items. If your health and shields are not at 100 percent, free up space in your backpack by consuming items that will replenish your HP and/or shields.

How to Collect Valuable Resources

Most points of interest on the map contain buildings, trees, rock formations, abandoned vehicles, and other pre-made structures. Buildings and structures can be explored and used to hide from enemies. Chests, weapons, ammo, and loot can often be found in buildings.

Just about any structure or item you encounter can be smashed with your pickaxe in order to gather resources. This includes the floors, walls and ceilings of buildings, the contents of buildings (including furniture, appliances, countertops, and items in stores), fences around buildings, cars, trucks, and other structures.

Almost every object in the game can be smashed and transformed into resources using the pickaxe. When you smash a car to collect metal, its alarm will often sound. The noise will attract attention, and help enemies determine your location.

Your soldier can use wood, brick (stone), and metal to quickly building protective walls, fortresses, stairs, and ramps (shown on the previous page). Particularly in the final minutes of a battle, building strong and tall fortresses is often essential. You must have enough resources on hand to accomplish this, so plan accordingly. Between 500 and 1000 wood, metal, and/or stone should be adequate for building a fortress when you enter into the final circle of a match.

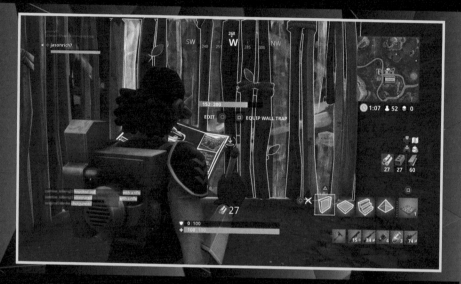

Throughout a match, quickly building a wall or box around yourself can protect you from enemy attacks, while building a ramp or bridge will help you quickly reach otherwise inaccessible areas.

In addition to using your pickaxe to collect resources, you can some-times find bundles of resources on the ground. When you see an icon for wood, bricks, or metal, be sure to pick them up. As you can see on the previous page, a brick (worth 30 stone) is waiting to be picked up by the soldier.

Keep in mind, your pickaxe can also be used as a short-range weapon, especially if the soldier you're fighting against is also unarmed except for their pickaxe.

To Stay Healthy, Maintain Your HP and Shields

Your wood, stone, and metal resource counters are always displayed on the screen during a match. Other useful information is also displayed, including your soldier's Health Meter and Shield Meter. Anytime you fall or get hit by a weapon, some of your HP gets depleted. This is measured in green on the HP meter. If you have active shields (displayed in blue), first your shields get depleted, and then your HP goes down when you get injured or attacked.

When your character's HP meter, shown in the bottom-center of the screen (unless you're playing on a smartphone or tablet), hits zero, he or she meets their demise. However, to help protect your soldier, you can [misplaced modifier] boost their HP, plus provide them with added protection with shields. This is shown on the previous page.

Be Sure to Collect Loot as You Explore

Just as powerful weapons and ammo can be found throughout the island, particularly in or near the various points of interest, a selection of loot is also available. Loot can help boost your HP, increase your shields, or provide additional weapons or tools that will help you stay alive. Epic Games continuously adds new types of loot to the game.

Descriptions of Loot Items

As of May 2018, the following is a list of loot you'll likely encounter on the island. Some items are considered rare, and much harder to find than others.

- **Apples**—These are found randomly under trees throughout the island. For each one your soldier consumes, their Health Meter increases by five.
- **Bandages**—Each time a Bandage is used, it replenishes 15 HP. A player can carry up to 5 bandages within their backpack in a single slot. It takes several seconds to use Bandages, during which time a soldier is vulnerable to attack, so be sure you're well-hidden or protected when using this item.
- **Boogie Bombs**—Toss one of these bombs at an opponent and they'll be forced to dance for 5 seconds while taking damage.
- **Bushes**—A bush can be worn by a soldier and used as camouflage. Be sure to crouch down to avoid being seen. If there are other bushes in the area, you'll blend right in. However, a bush offers no protection from attacks. If you start moving while camouflaged by a bush, an adversary will definitely notice and attack. This item is best used outside, when standing still, to avoid being detected by nearby enemies

- **Cozy Campfires**—Once the fire is activated, any soldiers who stand next to it will gain 2 HP per second for up to 25 seconds (up to 50 HP). The drawback is that a soldier is vulnerable to attack during this time, so activate the campfire after building a protective barrier around yourself and the campfire, or find a secure and secluded place to use it. If you're playing with teammates, multiple people can take advantage of the campfire's healing powers. When you stand next to the flame, look for the "+" icons that appear so you know it's working.

- **Chug Jugs**—This item takes 15 seconds to drink, during which time a soldier is vulnerable to attack unless he/she's protected. Consuming a Chug Jug restores a soldier's HP *and* Shield Meter to 100 percent. Drink one of these as you enter into later stages of a match, when survival becomes more difficult.

- **Clingers**—When you throw one of these plunger-shaped grenades at an enemy, it sticks to them and then explodes.

- **Grenades**—Toss a grenade at an enemy, and it'll explode on impact. Direct hits cause the most damage, but even if the grenade lands close to an enemy, damage is still inflicted.

- **Impulse Grenades**—This type of grenade inflicts damage to enemies and throws them into the air, away from the point of impact.

- **Launch Pads**—Activate this item to catapult your solider into the air, and then automatically deploy their glider. You can then guide them around in mid-air for a few seconds. Use this tool, for example, to escape after being engulfed by the storm, or to flee from an attack. It allows you to move great distances quickly. While you're flying, you can still be shot at by enemies. One item that periodically gets added to the game are Jetpacks. These too allow a solider to temporarily fly through the air to get around quickly, or to launch attacks from above.

- **Small Shield Potions**—Consuming this item increases your shield strength by 25, but it takes several seconds to drink, during which time your soldier is vulnerable to attack.

- **Med Kits**—Restore your health to 100 percent each time a Med Kit is used. It takes 10 seconds to use a Med Kit, during which time your solider is vulnerable to attack.

- **Port-A-Forts**—This insta-fort is made of metal, and instantly gets built when you activate it. Use it for protection without the need for manual building. It requires no resources. Use the surrounding tires to jump to the top of the fort with ease. In addition to offering protection, the top of a fort provides an ideal vantage point for sniping enemies.

- **Remote Explosives**—A soldier can carry up to 10 of these explosives at once. Activate by attaching it to an object, wall, or structure, and then detonate it remotely from any distance away. After setting up a remote explosive, lure your adversary to its location before detonating it. Just make sure you're far enough away to avoid the explosion yourself.

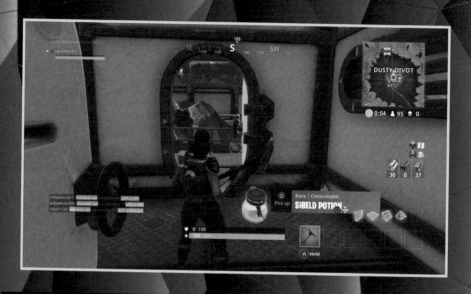

- **Shield Potions**—Each time you drink a Shield Potion, your Shield Meter increases by 50 (up to a maximum of 100). Drink two in a row to fully activate and replenish your soldier's shields. This item takes several seconds to consume, during which time your soldier is vulnerable to attack.

- **Slurp Juice**—As you drink this item (seen in the previous page), your HP and shield strength increases by one point every second for up to 25 seconds. While you're drinking, your soldier must be standing still and is vulnerable to attack.

- **Traps**—Set a Trap on any structure's floor, wall, or ceiling and then leave it. When an opponent accidently activates the hidden Trap, they'll receive mega-damage. Just make sure you don't set off the Trap yourself once you've activated it, or you'll be the one getting hurt! Shown here is a Trap waiting to be picked up and placed into the soldier's backpack for later use.

At least during Season 4, anytime you explore a crater, chances are you'll find **Hop Rocks**.

Consume one or more of these rocks, and for a short time, you will be able to jump higher and leap farther. You'll also be protected from harm as a result of a fall.

SECTION 2
GET ACQUAINTED WITH THE MAP

With the exception of your ride on the Battle Bus prior to landing on the island, just about all the action that transpires during *Fortnite: Battle Royale* takes place on the island itself. No matter how well you get to know the island, it continues to evolve as new points of interest are added by Epic Games and changes are made to the terrain.

Before boarding the bus, while you're exploring the pre-deployment area, be sure to access the island map to determine the direction and route the Battle Bus will be following. The pre-deployment area is shown above. This is where you hang out while other players are joining the game.

The blue line (composed of arrows) displayed across the map depicts the route and direction in which the Battle Bus will be flying. As you study this map, start thinking about your landing location. Do you want to land in a less popular and more secluded area, so you can gather weapons and resources, or would you prefer to drop down into a popular part of the island where you're sure to encounter enemy soldiers, and will be forced to engage in battles?

Find Your Way Using Map Coordinates

The full island map is divided into quadrants (boxes). Displayed along the top margin of the map (from left to right) are the letters "A" through "J." Along the left margin of the map, from top to bottom, are the numbers "1" through "10." Using these letters and numbers, you can easily identify any location or quadrant on the map.

For example, quadrant F2 on the map corresponds with Anarchy Acres, while section H6 corresponds with Retail Row. Lucky Landing can be found in quadrant G10. By studying the map, you'll discover that most, but not all, of the popular points of interest are listed.

Choose the Best Moment to Jump from the Battle Bus

At the start of each match, choose when to jump off the Battle Bus as it sails across the sky directly over the island.

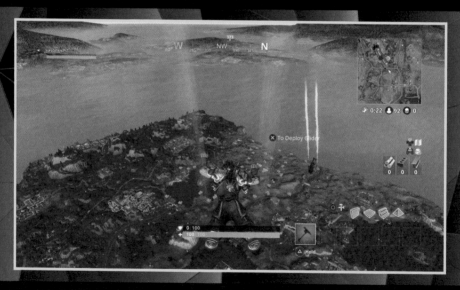

Once you depart the Battle Bus, your soldier free falls toward the island, but you can control the speed and direction in which they're falling. If you don't touch the controller, your soldier falls at a steady pace. Remember, the soldiers who make it safely to the ground first are at an advantage, because they can quickly grab a weapon and then start shooting unarmed adversaries as they land.

If you point your soldier in a downward direction during freefall, their falling speed increases dramatically, allowing them to reach land faster.

As your soldier gets closer to land, manually deploy their glider. Once a glider is active (seen on the previous page), it slows the soldier's rate of descent, and you have greater control over their direction. If you wait too long, the glider automatically deploys itself, ensuring a safe landing.

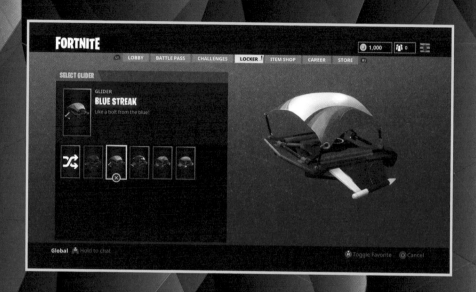

From the Item Shop, or by completing daily or weekly challenges within the game, unlock different glider designs. They all function the same way, however. Access the Locker (shown above), and after acquiring various gliders, choose which one to associate with your soldier. You can switch gliders, as well as your soldier's outfit and back bling, from the Locker before each match.

Need Directions? Check the Map

The small map that's continuously displayed on the screen, along with the full-sized map, both offer a lot of useful information when it comes to navigation and determining the safest places to go to avoid the deadly storm. You can see this on the next page.

Once you've landed on the island, a small version of the map, which shows your current location, is continuously displayed. It's found near the top-right corner of the screen, but its location will vary based on which gaming platform you're using.

When a white line appears within the small map, this is the path you should follow to avoid the moving storm. If you see a portion of the white circle on this small map, this indicates that you're close to the border of the uninhabitable area due to the storm. If you find yourself outside of this circle once the storm moves, it's not a good situation.

Using this map, figure out where you want to go next, as well as the best route to follow, based on the direction in which the storm is moving, and the area of the map you want to reach. The white circle on the map indicates where the safe area will be after the storm moves again and shrinks the area of the island that remains inhabitable.

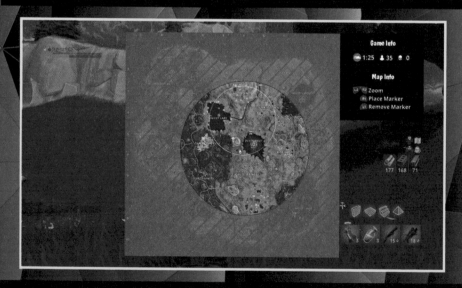

During a battle, access the full island map at any time. Use this version of the map to pinpoint the location of the storm and determine areas that are already uninhabitable due to the storm (displayed in pink on the map). Remember, the (inner white circle) indicates where the safe area will be once the storm expands again.

If you suddenly get defeated, don't despair. Stick around for a bit and take advantage of Spectator Mode. This allows you to kick back and watch other players compete in the match you were just eliminated from. Simply by watching other gamers explore, you'll learn a lot about various regions of the map, plus discover new strategies to use when engaged in fights.

SECTION 3
PREPARE FOR BATTLE

What type of *Fortnite* soldier do you want to become? Are you aggressive? Do you want to jump right into fights, defeating as many adversaries as possible as you make your way through each match?

The ultimate goal of *Fortnite: Battle Royale* is to be the last person alive at the end of each match. Up to 99 adversaries jump off the Battle Bus with you. Some get defeated early on, while others defend themselves successfully and manage to remain alive until the final circle, when the remaining players are forced into close proximity and must fight each other until only one person or team remains.

Instead of risking your life early on, perhaps your approach is to land in a less popular location, explore the island, and spend time collecting weapons, ammo, loot, and resources, while staying clear of enemy combatants until the storm forces you into close proximity with your enemies.

Whatever overall strategy you adopt during a battle, there are some fighting and maneuvering basics you'll definitely want to master. First, having quick reflexes is essential. Whether you're engaged in a gunfight or building your own structures (or fortresses), you need to be able to:

- Select, load, and aim a weapon quickly. In most gunfights, the soldier with the fastest trigger finger, the most powerful weapon, and the most accurate aim wins.
- Select a building material and building shape quickly, and then put the pieces together to construct the type of structure you need.
- Memorize the controller buttons (PS4 or Xbox One), keyboard and mouse buttons (Windows PC and Mac), or

screen taps (smartphones and tablets) that allow you to control your soldier with precision. While what can be done is the same across all gaming platforms, the actual controls are different, and often customizable, based on the gaming platform you're using.

Basic Strategies to Help You Maneuver and Stay Alive

The following are some basic strategies you'll need to master early on as a *Fortnite* noob (beginner). As you gain experience, build on these strategies, as you increase your speed and agility when fighting, building, and exploring the island.

Your soldier is able to walk, run, crouch down, tiptoe, or jump, while at the same time holding a pickaxe or weapon.

When crouched down, your soldier moves more slowly and becomes a smaller target. Crouching down also improves your aim when shooting and allows you to crawl under objects, such as partially open garage doors (shown here).

Crouching behind rocks, or other objects, or within a bush, can keep you hidden from nearby enemies.

Anytime you're out in the open, instead of walking or running in a straight line, continuously jump up and down and move in an unpredictable zigzag formation so you become a much more difficult target to hit.

Sometimes the fastest way down when you're standing on top of a cliff or structure is to jump down. Instead of jumping off of a cliff, which will often result in injury (a reduction of HP), slide down steep cliffs and hills.

To quickly reach the top of a structure, or instead of jumping down from a high up structure and risking injury, consider building a ramp.

You're often able to cross between the roofs or higher levels of buildings by constructing a bridge.

Be creative when using your building skills, so you can more easily approach difficult-to-reach [If it's inaccessible, it can't be approached] areas.

Be sure to collect resources as you move around the island, so you can build ramps, bridges, structures, and fortresses when you need them. Wooden structures offer the least protection but are the fastest to build. Building with stone or metal offers more defensive protection against attacks. Based on the resources you've collected, you can manually or automatically switch between wood, stone, or metal when in building mode.

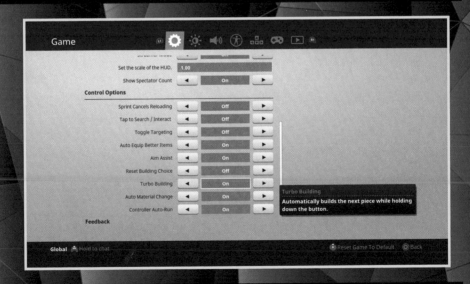

To speed up your building capabilities, be sure to adjust the game's Settings, and turn on features like Turbo Building and Auto Material Change.

Knowing that the attics of many buildings and structures contain chests and other loot, consider landing on top of buildings and then smashing through the roof with your pickaxe, or building a ramp from ground level outside a building directly to the roof.

If you approach a building and its door is already open, that means someone else has already explored that building and may still be inside. Listen for footsteps and be aware that the chests and other loot that were in the building likely will have been collected already. To trick your enemies, consider closing doors behind you after entering buildings, and then tiptoe around so you create the least amount of noise possible. When you're ready, launch a surprise attack on an enemy, or sneak up and ambush them from behind.

Sound Plays an Integral Part in the Game

The sounds you hear within the game can help you achieve success, so always listen carefully. For example, when an adversary is nearby, you'll hear their footsteps, especially when you're both inside a building. Plus, based on the sound of weapon fire, it's often possible to determine how far away you are from an enemy, and from which direction they're attacking.

If someone is collecting resources using their pickaxe, this, too, makes noise, especially if they're collecting metal by smashing cars or trucks. When you're the one collecting resources, make sure you're alone in the area. However, if you hear the sound of someone else collecting resources, this means they don't have a weapon in hand, so consider launching a sneak attack or using a projectile weapon, such as a grenade, to defeat them.

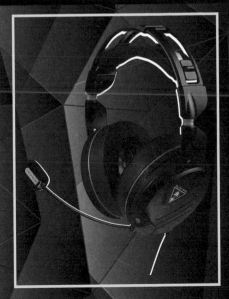

Use stereo headphones or a gamer's headset when playing *Fortnite*, so you can adjust the volume and hear every sound clearly.

SECTION 4
SURVIVING THE STORM

When you first land on the island, the entire landmass in safe to explore and fully inhabitable. However, the deadly storm slowly starts to move in, making large portions of the island uninhabitable. Ideally, you want to avoid getting stuck in the ever-moving and expanding storm.

Getting stuck in the storm causes your HP to decrease, slowly at first. The amount of damage inflicted will increase the longer you stay in the storm. Getting caught in the storm for too long will result in your demise. You'll also discover that your soldier walks and runs more slowly in the storm.

If you must enter the storm, make sure your Health and Shield meters are full, so you can withstand the harmful effects of the storm longer. One quick way to exit the storm is to utilize a Launch Pad, assuming you have one stored in your backpack.

As you're standing near the border of the storm (on the safe side), select a safe sniping position, and attack enemies as they exit the storm in search of safety. If you're the one exiting the storm, watch out for surprise attacks from enemies. Your current position is always indicated by a white arrow icon on the map.

Check the map to determine which portions of the island are already uninhabitable and avoid those areas.

One of the worst mistakes you can make is not paying attention to the storm. If you find yourself too far away from a safe area as the storm engulfs the area you're in, you may not be able to escape fast enough and will perish inside the storm. Notice this soldier's location (in the top-right corner of the map) compared to the safe circle.

Even running at top speed, escaping the storm can be difficult, if not impossible, without using a Launch Pad or Jetpack.

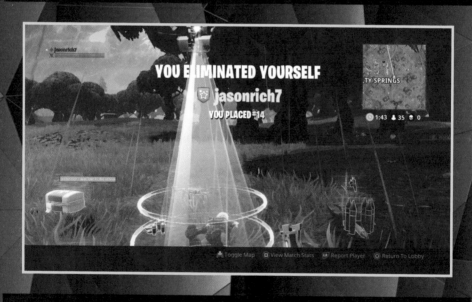

Throughout each battle, the white circle that's displayed on the map showcases the safe area of the island, based on the next move the storm will be making. Make your way toward the inside of the white circle while time permits.

Every few minutes, this circle of safe space contracts—sometimes dramatically. The on-screen timer will inform you about when the storm will once again expand and move. Listen for the sound of the timer's ticker and the approaching storm as it gets close. Warning messages will also appear near the center of the screen (shown here).

As a match progresses, the size of the circle shrinks until all the remaining soldiers are forced into a relatively small area in which they'll engage in their final battles for survival. By the time you reach this final circle, be sure to have plenty of resources on hand to build tall and strong fortresses. Also, make sure you have projectile weapons, such as a grenade launcher and/or a sniper rifle, with plenty of ammo at your disposal.

SECTION 5

ADJUST YOUR FIGHTING STRATEGIES BASED ON LOCATION

In *Fortnite: Battle Royale*, the fighting strategy you adopt should be based on five key factors:

1. The weapons and ammo currently in your arsenal.
2. The resources you have available to build a fortress, protective barriers, or ramps/stairs to get higher than your opponent(s).
3. The number of adversaries you'll be facing and which weapons they appear to have at their disposal.
4. Your location on the map.
5. Your experience playing the game, and how well you've fine-tuned your muscle memory when it comes to aiming and firing weapons or building structures.

You'll discover that scattered throughout the island, as well as in chests, Vending Machines, and supply drops, for example, are many different types of weapon. Some are rare, and far more powerful than others. Some weapons come with limited ammo, while others don't inflict too much damage to an enemy with each direct hit.

Some types of weapons, such as pistols or even your pickaxe are ideal for close-range fighting. Most types of rifles and mid-sized weapons are suited for mid-range fights. When using most types of weapons, it'll take multiple shots to defeat an enemy, as opposed to simply causing damage. Making a headshot, as opposed to a body shot, always inflicts the most damage, or allows for a one-shot win, depending on the weapon being used.

Weapons with a scope or projectile weapons (such as grenade launchers) are much better suited for long-range sniping and fighting. These long-range weapons should be saved until the final stages of a battle, when the circle is small, and the remaining soldiers are all within a specific fighting area.

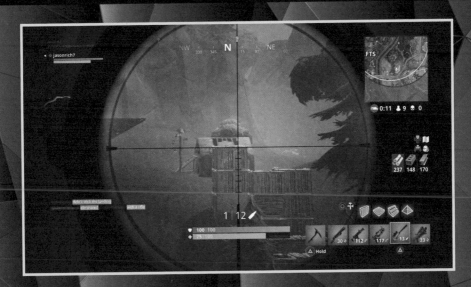

If a weapon has a scope or the ability to aim, activate it to improve your shooting accuracy. Regardless of the weapon you're using, if you crouch down when you shoot, your aim and accuracy improves.

Walking or running while shooting results in poor aim, so try to avoid this. However, when you're in close proximity to an enemy, you'll need to keep moving while shooting to avoid getting hit yourself.

Unarmed, but under attack? Grab your pickaxe, move in super close to your adversary, and keep smashing away. It'll take a bunch of direct hits to defeat an enemy, but if you keep moving around (making yourself a tough target to hit), and keep your pickaxe slashing away, you can win a battle, especially if the opponent is also unarmed.

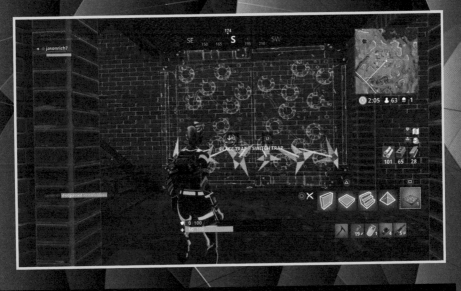

Depending on the situation, Boogie Bombs, Clingers, Grenades, Impulse Grenades, Remote Explosives, and Traps (shown here) can be useful weapons, but you need to determine the most opportune time to use each of them, assuming they're within your arsenal. Weapons like Boogie Bombs, Clingers, or Grenades are ideal when you're in close proximity to your enemy, or you're above your enemy and can drop a weapon down on them. Weapons like Remote Explosives and Traps need to be set up in advance, so plan accordingly.

Located around Dusty Divot, as well as other craters caused by falling comets in Season 4, you'll discover Hop Rocks. Once your soldier consumes one of these, his/her body will start to glow.

For about 30 seconds after consuming a Hop Rock, your soldier will be able to jump extra high and cover extra distance when quickly leaping forward. Use this to jump toward an enemy from far away and launch a surprise attack. You can also cover a lot of territory and move to another location using a series of successive leaps.

It's absolutely essential that you practice using various types of weapons so you're prepared to fight, launch attacks, or just protect yourself, in a variety of situations. Be sure to arrange your backpack so your most versatile and powerful weapons are easily accessible.

Use the Terrain to Your Advantage

The island offers many different types of terrain that will impact your ability to launch attacks, protect yourself, hide, find weapons and loot, and/or gather resources. Use the terrain you're in to your advantage whenever possible.

Finding yourself out in the open can be dangerous, especially if there are areas where enemies armed with a sniper rifle (or scoped weapon) can be hidden above you. In this situation, keep running, continually jump, and be prepared to quickly build walls or a small fortress to protect yourself as needed.

Whether you're inside or outside, if you're on the offensive, get to the higher ground, so you're above your enemies. This makes it easier to shoot downwards to attack them. The soldier who is closest to the ground is typically at a disadvantage. Here, when an adversary walks into the room below, they can be shot on sight, and probably won't think to look up.

Buildings and pre-made structures are typically chock-full of weapons, ammo, and loot. Inside these structures, you'll always find secure areas to hide. Remember, it's easier to hear your enemies approaching while inside buildings. As you can see on the previous page, you can always build within structures to better secure your position and defend yourself. Here, a wall was built to block off a hallway inside of a house, so the next room could be explored without worrying about someone sneaking up from behind.

If you're in an area where other soldiers are present, once you enter a building, close the door behind you (to cover your tracks), collect the weapons, ammo, and loot, and then find the corner of a room, or a space behind furniture to hide. Prepare to launch a surprise ambush on enemies as they walk into the room you're hiding in. Just make sure your back and sides are secure, so nobody can sneak up on you or shoot you through a nearby window.

As you're about to enter a building or pre-made structure, pause by the entrance and listen carefully for footsteps or noises coming from inside. Be sure to peak through a window, if possible, to see if anyone's lurking inside. You can always shoot an enemy through a window, even from far away when using a scoped weapon.

Since being higher than an opponent gives you a fighting advantage, it's often safer to land on the roof of a building as you're exiting the Battle Bus, to build a ramp from the ground to the outside roof of a building, or to build a bridge between the roofs of two buildings, and then use your pickaxe to smash your way through the roof and into the attic or top floor of the building or structure.

Smash through the ceiling and then work your way down as you clear each floor of enemies, while collecting the weapons, ammo, and loot you come across. If you enter the front door of a building and climb up the stairs, for example, an enemy could be waiting from a better vantage point to fire their weapon.

In Loot Lake and other areas of the island, you'll often need to travel across water. Walking (or attempting to run) through water is a slow process, and it leaves you out in the open, vulnerable to attack. Instead, build a wooden bridge to quickly cross lakes and rivers.

Each time you enter a new point of interest on the map, consider making your way to the highest point you can reach, or build a tall ramp to get a bird's-eye view of the area (as seen on the previous page). Using the scope of a weapon in your arsenal, look around for enemy movement, figure out where you want to go, and determine the safest route to take without becoming overly exposed.

Exploring narrow tunnels and confined (often underground) areas is required when you visit points of interest like Shifty Shafts or the base in Dusty Divot. Proceed through these areas with your weapon drawn and tiptoe, so you make the least sound possible. You never know who will be waiting as you make a sharp turn.

Some areas, like Wailing Woods (shown on the previous page) and Moisty Mire, offer an abundance of resources (including wood), but fewer weapons, ammo, and chests can be found here then in other points of interest. Thus, unless the storm forces players into these areas, they tend to be less popular and safer to explore. As you make your way through these areas, use the trees and natural surroundings for cover and protection.

Abandoned trucks often contain chests, weapons, or ammo within them. Once you collect the loot, if you think another soldier is nearby and will want to search the same truck soon, put your back against the truck's inside wall, crouch down, aim your weapon toward the truck's door, and prepare to launch an attack. As soon as you see someone attempt to enter the truck, fire your weapon!

SECTION 6
EXPLORING THE ISLAND LOCATION BY LOCATION

The island includes more than 20 main points of interest. Between each point of interest is typically open land (offering different types of terrain, like valleys, mountains, or dense forest areas) that you'll need to travel across to go from one location to the next as the circle gets smaller due to the storm.

Located in close proximity to some points of interest are additional areas to explore, although they're not labeled on the map. What's important to understand is that the island is continually evolving as new updates are made to the game.

Just when you think you've memorized the layout of a particular region, like Snobby Shores, the game designers add new structures or change the point of interest enough to make it seem totally new. This continual evolution of the island is one of the key ingredients that continues to make playing *Fortnite: Battle Royale* both fun and challenging.

This section focuses on highlights worth exploring within each point of interest. However, while the gameplay strategies described will remain the same, the terrain and what you encounter when you explore the island will definitely change over time.

If you're playing *Fortnite: Battle Royale* in Fall 2018 or beyond, chances are that when you look at the island map, you'll discover new points of interest that are not featured in this unofficial strategy guide, because

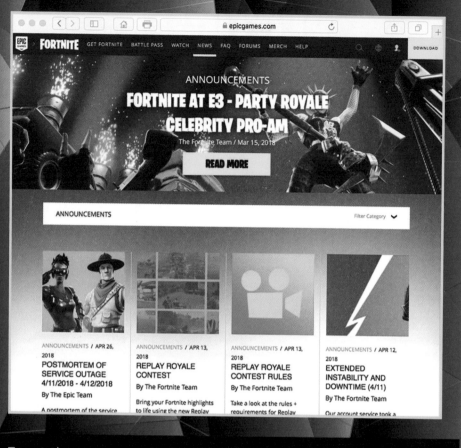

To get the scoop on what's new within the game, be sure to visit the game's official website (www.epicgames.com/fortnite/en-US/news) for the latest news about the game. Alternatively, visit one of the websites, YouTube Channels, Twitch channels, or other online resources that are featured in "Section 8: *Fortnite* Resources."

Anarchy Acres: Enjoy the Farm Life (While It Lasts)

Welcome to the farmland area of the island, where you'll come across barns, silos, tractors, and wilted crop fields, along with anything but peace and quiet. Sorry, everyone's favorite farmer, Old McDonald, does not live here!

When enemy troops are in the area, instead of hearing the moo of cows or the oink of pigs, you'll likely hear the sound of gunfire and grenade explosions. Here a bang, there a bang, everywhere a bang, bang! On the map, Anarchy Acres is found near coordinates F3.

The large farmhouse (shown here) and barn are where you'll find the best collection of weapons, ammo, and loot, although you won't be too disappointed if you explore the smaller structures as well.

When something you're looking for is hard to find, you've probably heard the expression, "It's like finding a needle in a haystack." Well, in Anarchy Acres, searching the haystacks by smashing them with your pickaxe or shooting at them will sometimes reveal useful loot. Haystacks also make great hiding places, but provide zero defense against incoming bullets (shown on the previous page).

The large barn contains several levels. Be sure to check the top level, as well as any areas that are difficult to reach, to find the best loot. You're safer staying higher up, so you can shoot downward at enemies.

In the stable (shown on the previous page), you'll find goodies on the ground in many of the stalls. Build a ramp to reach the second level, where you'll discover a chest.

Don't be surprised if you're not alone in the stables. When you hear someone approaching, find an object to crouch down behind, draw a weapon, and prepare to defend yourself.

In the farmhouse, as well as the barn and stable, you're apt to find chests, if you look hard enough (like the one on the previous page).

It's often a good distance between buildings and structures within Anarchy Acres. When you need to cross open land, run fast, jump often, and follow an unpredictable zig-zag path. If you see and hear gunfire that's aimed at you, look for an object to hide behind, or quickly build a wall or mini-fortress for protection.

Dusty Divot: Explore the Crater and the Base That's Now Located Here

Near the dead-center of the island is what's now known as Dusty Divot. You'll find it near map coordinates G5. This area was redesigned in Season 4, when comets fell onto the island. What this area will become in the future remains unknown, so if you visit here in Summer 2018 or later, Dusty Divot could be totally different.

In the center of the massive crater is a base that contains many rooms and tunnels to explore. Outside the base, the terrain is covered with Hop Rocks. As one of the newest areas on the map, and thanks to its

central location, Dusty Divot is not only one of the most popular locations on the island, it also becomes part of many battle circles as the
storm closes in.

If you land here, you will get defeated quickly unless you grab a weapon
to defend yourself. Consuming Hop Rocks makes soldiers able to jump
higher and quickly leap farther. This can definitely be used by you (or
your enemies) as a tactical advantage when fighting.

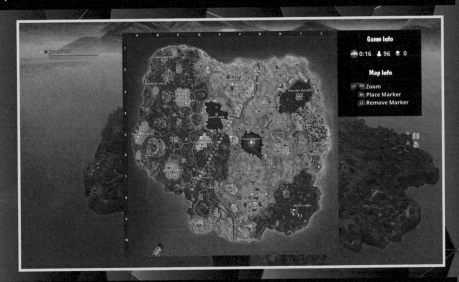

The route many Battle Buses travel goes directly over Dusty Divot (or
close to it).

Located on the outskirts of the crater are the remains of two warehouses (shown in the previous page). Inside, you'll be able to grab some chests, weapons, ammo, and loot. The problem is, if you're not one of the first to arrive here, you'll be shot within seconds of approaching.

The main base area in the center of the crater is comprised of multiple compartments that are connected by tunnels. If you land directly on the roof of the base, smash your way through the ceiling to enter.

Inside the base, you never know what to expect behind each door (like the one seen on the previous page). There may be an enemy soldier waiting to attack, or a lab that contains a chest or other useful items.

If you manage to make your way to the center of the secret base, you'll discover that research is being done on the comet that fell to the island (which caused the massive crater). Be sure to explore around here, but once again, watch out for enemy soldiers. They're probably everywhere!

Located near the corner of the base is this watchtower (shown on the previous page). Inside, you'll find a chest. The top of this tower offers a good vantage point from which to use a sniper rifle to shoot at your enemies.

Fatal Fields: Where Old McDonald Goes to Fight, Not Farm

This is another of the island's farming regions. Located at map coordinates G8.5, the area includes [to avoid misplaced modifier] a large farmhouse, several barns, stables, and many fields of wilted crops. The larger buildings tend to have the most loot, but these are also where all of the region's visitors explore first, so don't expect to be alone here.

The first thing you'll notice is that Fatal Fields covers a lot of territory. Second, each building is located a good distance from the others, which means you'll need to run across open terrain and be vulnerable to attack as you move from structure to structure. Be ready to build a protective shield as you're running.

The large barn has several levels to explore. The bundles and piles of hay serve as great places to hide, so watch out for hidden enemies. Behind hay, you may also find loot, however.

Inside the stables, be sure to check each horse stall for ammo, loot, and weapons. Build a ramp to reach the second level, where you'll find a chest. Also check the two large silos located on the farm. You'll find a chest and loot inside at least one of them.

The farmhouse is very much like the homes you'll explore elsewhere on the island. It comprises multiple floors, each with several rooms. In many of the rooms, you're apt to find chests, weapons, ammo, and/ or loot. Of course, behind any closed door, an enemy soldier could be waiting to ambush you, so proceed with caution.

Make your way through the bathroom in the farmhouse, and you'll discover a hidden room containing a chest.

Flush Factory: Don't Get Wiped When Exploring This Toilet Factory

You'll encounter toilets everywhere as you explore this now abandoned factory. In addition to the factory floor, there are a handful of offices, bathrooms, truck loading areas, and other places to navigate through.

Located a short distance from Flush Factory (found at map coordinates E9) is an unmarked area of the map that contains a cluster of buildings, one of which is a dance club. As always, when you discover enemy soldiers in the area, being higher offers an advantage. Try to avoid areas of the toilet factory that leave you out in the open and vulnerable, then insert your own poop jokes here.

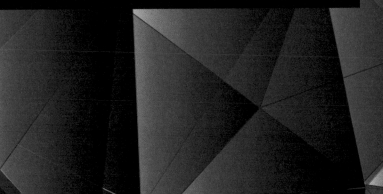

The main factory area of Flush Factory can be found at map coordinates D9.5.

Step inside the factory to find machinery, conveyor belts, and a handful of tiny rooms. You can walk along the conveyor belts, build ramps, or find stairs to reach higher levels.

You will need to build stairs or a ramp to reach certain areas of the factory, such as above this restroom, where you'll find a chest.

The front office of the factory features a toilet display. While this is useless to you, look around for some weapons, ammo, and loot on the ground.

Either before or after exploring Flush Factory, take a short walk to the cluster of buildings located nearby.

he building with the red ropes in front contains a dance club. This area as added to the game in Season 4. It has become the area's most popar fight and dance spot. Listen for the music as you approach.

n the dance floor showcase some of your dance moves, or work your ay up to the DJ booth. Be sure to explore the outskirts of this building nd the rooms you'll discover as you leave the dance floor.

Check behind the DJ booth to find a chest, and then face the dance floor and spin some tunes.

The other buildings in this area all offer useful loot to discover. Smash through the outside wall of this building that's located next to the dance club, and you'll find a chest.

Stake out an area that overlooks the entrance to the dance club, and then shoot at enemy soldiers as they go in or out. A sniper rifle works best, but any long-range weapon will do the trick if you aim properly.

Parked outside of the buildings in the unlabeled cluster of buildings are a handful of trucks and metal containers. Check inside these vehicles and containers for chests and useful loot. If you crouch down within the back of a truck, this will serve as decent shielding from an incoming attack. Smashing the trucks with your pickaxe will generate metal.

Another useful item found near the new cluster of buildings is a Vending Machine. Use it to stock up on any additional weapons you may need, assuming you have enough loot to use as payment.

Greasy Grove: Discover Food, Shops, and Homes to Explore

Located at map coordinates C7, Greasy Grove is home to a few fast food restaurants, stores, and homes that contain chests, weapons, ammo, and other useful loot. There is also a handful of abandoned vehicles and some chain link fencing which you're able to smash with your pick-axe in order to collect metal. Trees (for collecting wood) can be found mainly in the outskirts of this relatively small area, but the buildings themselves can be smashed in order to gather wood and stone.

If you plan to make Greasy Grove your landing destination upon leaving the Battle Bus, you can get a lovely bird's-eye view of the area as you land. Consider landing on the roof of one of the larger homes, and then smashing your way into the attic to quickly find some goodies.

As always, once inside a home, look under the staircases for useful loot. Here, an ammo box was discovered.

The cars in the parking lot can be smashed in order to collect metal. Vehicle alarms will go off, so make sure you're the only one in the area when you start smashing away with your pickaxe.

Don't just search inside the homes. Inside this doghouse you'll find a chest. Smash apart the doghouse, and the chest will be waiting for you to open it.

The attics and basements of the homes are worth exploring as well. You may not always find a chest, but other loot can typically be discovered, such as this Cozy Campfire.

Inside the sporting goods shop, random loot will likely be lying on the ground waiting to be snatched up, but don't forget to check behind the counters as well.

Look inside these fenced-in areas. Not only are the fences and machinery great sources of metal, you'll typically find powerful weapons and ammo on the ground waiting to be grabbed.

Behind the stone structure located next to the burger shop, you'll discover this Vending Machine. Make sure you have at least 300 wood, stone, or metal on hand to purchase some loot.

Check Out the Nearby Sports Complex

Follow the path out of Greasy Grove toward map coordinates C5 to discover a sports complex that contains several buildings.

While not labeled on the island map as a point of interest, this sports complex includes an indoor soccer field and an indoor swimming pool. Shown here is a soldier standing on the roof of the pool.

Smash through the pool building's ceiling to collect metal and reach this empty swimming pool area. You'll likely discover weapons or ammo on the pool floor. (seen on the previous page)

The car and truck stuck in the empty pool are a great source of metal, so start smashing.

Check the locker rooms and behind counters to discover weapons, ammo, and loot on the ground (shown on the previous page). You may also discover ammo boxes on shelves.

Within the indoor soccer arena you'll find a massive field. Kicking the soccer ball around is fun, but won't help you stay alive. Instead, check the goalie nets for goodies, then explore the rooms and areas surrounding the field.

Outside the soccer arena is a Vending Machine (shown on the previous page). This one offers Med Kits that cost 200 stone each.

Haunted Hills: Forget the Ghosts, Watch Out for Enemy Soldiers

Ghosts are not the thing to be afraid of when you enter this region of the island, located at map coordinates B3. What you'll find here are old churches, creepy crypts, an eerie graveyard, and some small stone mausoleums (that often contain loot).

You're likely to encounter many enemies here. If you need to engage in gun battles, there are plenty of stone objects, like tombstones, to crouch behind and use for cover. This is not a particularly large area, and it's surrounded by large mountains. There are roads, however, that lead to Junk Junction and Snobby Shores, when you're ready to leave.

There are two churches here. Be sure to explore all levels of each of them, including the towers and basements.

Check inside the small stone mausoleums as well, especially if you're looking to stock up on weapons and ammo.

If you're the first to explore the graveyard areas, you'll often find weapons and loot lying on the ground, out in the open.

Inside the churches, smash through stone walls to find hidden chambers and crypts, and sometimes some useful loot as well.

One of the churches has a tall tower. Land on it (or build a ramp up to the top of it), and then smash your way down, and you'll likely find some worthwhile items.

As you'd expect, chests can be found inside the churches, both out in the open and within hidden chambers.

Sniping enemies is a good way to neutralize their threat. Look for high-up places where you can get a great view as your adversaries enter or exit a structure. Aim your weapon, and then wait for the perfect moment to fire.

Junk Junction: There's More Than a Whole Lotta Trash Here

This rather large junkyard offers a maze-like design which makes participating in fire fights here rather interesting because there are so many places to hide. There are also plenty of junk piles to climb, so you can reach higher ground and attack enemies from above. Junk Junction is located between map coordinates B1.5 and C1.5.

One of the tallest landmarks on the island is located just outside of Junk Junction.

From the Battle Bus, land on top of this llama and smash your way down.

As you work your way down the llama-shaped tower, you'll discover chests and plenty of other weapons, ammo, and loot.

Between the piles of smashed cars and trash are walkways. As you make your way through this maze-like area, watch for surprises from enemies around every turn, as well as from above. It's safer to build a ramp to the top of a junk pile, and then jump from pile to pile (or build a bridge), so you can stay in the high ground.

Be sure to peek into large metal canisters. You'll likely find useful weapons, ammo, loot, and/or a chest inside.

This is the view from the area's largest building. Look on top of the junk piles for useful items, and then be sure to explore inside the building.

From the roof, one of the two doors leads to a storeroom. Inside, you'll find random loot, or perhaps a chest.

In between piles of cars and junk, consider placing a Trap. When an unsuspecting adversary walks past the Trap, they'll get a painful surprise.

Located just outside of Junk Junction (near map coordinates C1), you'll discover this large building, as well as a few smaller structures. Search inside for useful items but check out the perimeter of the large building as well.

Behind the large building, you'll find smaller stone buildings that are worth exploring. Again, you never know what awesomeness is waiting inside for you to grab. Just be mindful of enemies who could be hiding nearby, so keep your close- or mid-range weapon drawn, and be ready to shoot.

Lonely Lodge: Camping Can Be Fun, When You're Not Being Shot At

The most exciting thing in this area (map coordinates J6) is a giant water-front mansion. It contains many rooms, most of which offer something worth grabbing. The rest of Lonely Lodge is made up of campgrounds, cabins, parked RVs, and a tall observation tower.

The mansion you'll find near Lonely Lodge is one of the largest on the island.

pproach the front door of the mansion (shown on the previous page)
nd smash the ground to discover a hidden basement. This is no ordi-
ary mansion! You'll quickly discover that it's some type of high-tech
ontrol center and hideout that contains an abundance of chests, weap-
ns, and ammo.

he basement levels of the mansion contain a top-secret, high-tech
ideout. Chests, weapons, and ammo are in abundance here, so look
arefully.

Seen on the previous page is one of several loot-filled chests you'll find in the basement levels of the mansion.

The main levels of the mansion are also chock-full of rooms that contain weapons, ammo, and loot, as well as great places to hide in order to ambush enemies.

Most of Lonely Lodge (found around map coordinates J5 and seen on the previous page) is comprised of heavily wooded areas with a stream running through much of it. As you walk around, you'll discover small structures, like cabins, to peek into.

The tallest structure in Lonely Lodge is this wooden observation tower. At the top, you'll find a chest and other loot, and get a spectacular view of the terrain below. If you have a sniper rifle, it's relatively easy to position yourself on the tower and then shoot at enemies from above. Whatever you do, don't fall or jump off the top of this tower or you'll perish.

Be sure to check out all levels of this lodge.

Once inside the lodge, go upstairs. There's a chest to be found, but you'll need to build a platform to reach it.

There are numerous small cabins to explore. Some contain useful items. These are great places to hide, wait for enemies to enter, and then launch an ambush. Another strategy is to set Traps or Remote Explosives in one or more of these cabins, and then wait for unsuspecting and curious enemy soldiers to enter.

Loot Lake: Take a Swim, Shoot an Enemy, Collect Some Loot

Perhaps the most picturesque location on the island is Loot Lake. However, just because it's pretty doesn't mean it's safe! Located at map coordinates E4, the main places you want to visit in this area include a small island that contains a home, a rowboat in the middle of the lake, and two buildings (near docks) located on the shoreline. Once you've seen the sights here, it's just a short run to Tilted Towers.

When nobody is around, navigating your way around Loot Lake is relatively easy. However, things get tricky and dangerous if there happen to be enemy soldiers in the vicinity.

If your destination after leaving the Battle Bus is Loot Lake, you have a few potential landing sites. If you notice the area isn't too crowded with enemy soldiers, consider landing on the island with the large house.

The large house on the island has several levels, and within it you'll discover plenty of weapons, ammo, and loot. Plus, this island offers a lot of resources (especially wood) to collect. To make your way to land, you can walk through water (which is slow and leaves you vulnerable), or you can build a wooden bridge and run to safely without being exposed for too long.

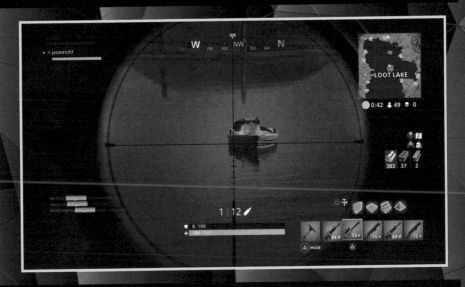

Notice that in the middle of the lake, there is a rowboat that contains a chest. If snipers are nearby, reaching this boat could be dangerous. If you're the sniper, wait for an enemy to reach this chest, and take the shot to end that soldier.

Should you manage to reach the boat safely, open the chest. If you've built a bridge to reach the boat, you can continue extending the bridge in order to reach the shore. However, if you walked through the water to reach the boat, you'll need to continue walking.

From the shoreline of Loot Lake (when standing on the docks), you'll notice two buildings. As you approach either building, watch for snipers and enemies hidden behind barriers who are waiting to jump out and attack, perhaps with a gun or a grenade. When you explore the smaller building on the left, you'll discover at least one chest, plus additional loot.

Enter the smaller building either through its front door or by crouching down and entering through the garage (which makes less noise, if you tiptoe).

Look around for the chest hidden behind some crates.

The second building comprises several floors. As you'd expect, a chest can be found on the top floor, although random loot can be found elsewhere. If you have a sniper rifle, the windows on the higher levels are ideal for peeking out from and spotting enemies to shoot at.

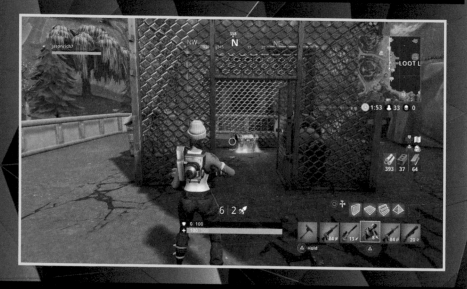

After climbing the stairs inside the building, to reach this loft area in the building, you'll need to build a ramp or additional stairs.

Climb the ramp you built to reach the loft.

Look for the chest behind some crates in the small loft space.

Located outside the buildings, you'll see a fenced-in area. Here you'll discover yet another chest.

Lucky Landing: Home of the Giant Pink Tree

As the Battle Bus is flying high in the sky, it's easy to spot Lucky Landing, because located in the center of this region is a giant pink tree that can easily be seen from above. Plus, many of the roofs of the Asian-inspired buildings are red.

The building with the giant pink tree in the middle of it is definitely a landmark worth visiting. You're likely to find some powerful and rare weapons here.

If you're approaching by land, you'll need to cross over a bridge that's also inspired by Asian architecture. On the bridge (as well as under it), you'll find chests and other loot.

In this Asian temple located slightly outside of Lucky Landing, there's a chest waiting for you in the main room.

On the side of this building you'll find a Vending Machine. Both inside Lucky Landing and on its outskirts, there are plenty of areas to collect wood, stone, and metal.

Climb to the top floor of this building and grab a sniper rifle (if you have one). As you explore the building, you will find useful items here.

Use the upstairs office window as a perch to snipe enemy soldiers below. If you have a long-range rifle without a scope, it'll work fine too.

You'll have even greater accuracy if you use a sniper rifle.

Just about every building in Lucky Landing has something worth grabbing inside.

Behind the counter, you'll find a chest in this building.

Moisty Mire: A Forest with a Few Surprises

This point of interest on the island is really two unique destinations in one. Near map coordinates H8, you'll discover the ruins of a prison, which is loaded with chests, weapons, ammo, and a few other surprises. There's also the main area of Moisty Mire, found around map coordinates I9, in the center of a forest. Here, there's an abandoned movie set that includes several buildings and movie set areas to explore, as well as some gooey swamp and lake terrain.

The forest area of Moisty Mire is a great place to stock up on wood. You'll need extra resources if you want to make purchases from the Vending Machine you'll find in the prison area. A short jog from the movie set area, you'll find this decrepit home. Inside are a chest and other useful items to be grabbed.

In the prison area, start by landing on or climbing up the guard towers. There are chests and plenty of other loot to be found here. Next, make your way through the other prison areas.

One of the roads that runs near the prison has a bunch of vehicles. These two chests offer a quick way to pick up some weapons and loot. Just around the corner from these cars is a Vending Machine. If you want to escape this prison alive, you'll need to be heavily armed and ready for battle.

You definitely want to check out the prison cells as you make your way through each area of the prison. Many cells have weapons and ammo on the ground waiting to be grabbed. During Season 4, the center of the prison contained a crater from a fallen comet. Here, you may discover Hop Rocks, which allow you to jump higher and leap farther. Whether or not the falling comet situation will be cleared up after Season 4 (Summer 2018) is anyone's guess.

In the movie set/swamp area, the treehouse offers a location from which to perch yourself and shoot at enemies below. You'll also find a chest. Just be careful on your approach, since you'll need to walk through open swamp terrain to access this treehouse from most directions.

One of the few actual buildings in the movie set area is craft services, where they feed the movie's cast and crew. As you can see on the previous page, there's a chest to be found here, as well as other useful loot.

The movie set area of Moisty Mire offers several interesting areas to wander through, as well as plenty of places to hide or launch a surprise attack from. Keep your eyes and ears peeled for chests and for enemies approaching from all sides.

In the middle of the swamp is a rowboat (seen on the previous page). In it is a chest. To reach the boat, you'll need to venture into an open area, plus walk through swampy water, which is a slow process. Consider building a bridge to get here faster, and be ready to build walls for shielding if you get attacked trying to reach the boat.

Pleasant Park: Suburbia at Its Finest

Pleasant Park is a rather large suburban region of the island that contains a bunch of single-family homes, a park, and a sports field. It's located at map coordinates C3. If you enjoy close-range gun fights, this is the place to visit, as it's always crowded. If you land here from the Battle Bus, and you don't locate and grab a weapon within seconds, you'll be defeated very quickly. This area is surrounded by a few small hills, as well as pathways and roads that lead to neighboring island hotspots.

You're sure to encounter numerous enemies here in Pleasant Park. Since you'll likely be fighting in tight spaces inside homes, be sure to have a pistol or another short-range weapon on hand.

The soccer field in the middle of town will likely offer a chest or other goodies. However, running into the middle of the field (or landing there) with no cover can be dangerous. Wait until you're sure the area is clear or be ready to build walls for shielding. If you're the second or third person to land in the field, the first soldier who lands will grab the available weapon(s), and the rest will be shot within moments of landing here.

The structure in the center of town offers a great view from the roof, and below you'll likely find a chest or other items worth collecting (seen on the previous page). But there's a lot of open space between the other structures and this one, so if Pleasant Park is filled with enemy soldiers, approach this location with caution, and be prepared to fight your way in and out of it.

If you land on the ceiling of a home and smash your way through the roof, keep in mind that some attics are compartmentalized, so you'll also need to smash your way through a few walls to reach all of the hidden rooms in an attic. Then, you may need to smash through the floor to reach the main areas of the house.

If you don't land on the roof of a home, build a ramp up to a roof and then smash your way into the attic with your pickaxe (as seen in the previous page).

There are two gas stations in the area. One is directly in Pleasant Park (which contains little that's of interest), and another is located just outside of the town. If you land in this more remote area and explore the second gas station, gather a few weapons and resources, and then take the approximately 30-second jog into town and start exploring the homes. This way, you enter Pleasant Park nicely armed and with some resources that you've collected. Check the roof of the second gas station, as well as its interior, to collect everything that's available.

Sometimes, you can gain the element of surprise if you enter into a house from the backdoor, especially if someone is already inside (seen on the previous page). Tiptoe to avoid being heard as you enter, although the enemy may hear the door opening.

If you're able to find and grab a few Traps, set them inside the houses in places that will surprise your enemies. Once they're set, close the nearby doors, and then hide somewhere at a distance or continue exploring. Chances are, one or more of your enemies will accidently stumble into your Trap, and then BOOM!

Anytime you see a home with a cellar door outside, be sure to smash it open and enter the basement. There's almost always a chest hidden somewhere in the cellar. Some cellars have multiple rooms, so grab whatever you see in each of them.

Outside doghouses, located next to homes, are sometimes great spots for finding hidden chests. Look for the golden glow.

The insides of most homes look the same. Lying on the floor, behind furniture, or under staircases, you'll sometimes find weapons, ammo, and loot. Explore each room, but always listen carefully for enemies that may be lurking around. Homes offer many great hiding places, and once an enemy has chosen a hiding spot and is standing still, they won't make any noise to give away their position.

Retail Row: You Won't Shop 'Til You Drop, But You May Drop from a Shot

When it comes to shopping on the island, Retail Row is the place to go. This area contains a handful of shops, restaurants, a water tower, and a few homes, most of which surround street parking areas. On the map, you'll find Retail Row at coordinates H6.

One of the more unique things about Retail Row is that the chests are not always in the same exact locations, but there are some places where chests are more apt to be found.

As with all points of interest, even if the route the Battle Bus takes does not travel directly over Retail Row, you can glide more than halfway across the map before your soldier's glider automatically deploys, so you can almost always reach this or any other area on the map.

Use your ability to control your soldier's freefall to guide him/her to your intended destination.

There are several good places to land in Retail Row, such as on top of the water tower, where you'll sometimes discover a chest.

Another good landing spot is on the roof of a home that's located toward the edge of the shopping region (shown on the previous page). This one is missing some of its roof, and from the right angle, you can see a chest in the attic below.

The cars in the parking areas make good cover to duck behind if you're getting shot at, or you can use the pickaxe to smash them and collect metal. Of course, you want to check in the backs of trucks first and make sure there's no loot that's worth grabbing.

Some of the shops and restaurants have loot that's clearly visible on the ground (shown on the previous page), but you'll often need to search for hidden rooms or hard-to-reach areas to find the best items.

In this market, look for the loading dock door, and enter through it.

Jump up onto a few cartons to discover a chest on the shelving near the ceiling.

Sometimes, the best way to reach the top of a building is to build a ramp from the ground to the roof using resources you've collected. Getting higher up than your enemies also gives you a bird's eye view of the area, plus it makes it easy to target those who are running around below you.

There are many buildings and structures to explore, but a lot of empty space to cross in order to reach them. Instead of putting yourself out in the open and running around in front of the buildings, consider traveling behind the buildings and taking the longer route around. This will take more time, but is often safer, especially if there are a lot of enemy soldiers running around this area.

Risky Reels: Tonight's Movie Is "Drive-In Shootout"

This drive-in movie theater can be found at map coordinates H2. Because it's new, it tends to be popular, so go in heavily armed, or if you're landing here from the Battle Bus, grab a weapon quickly.

Risky Reels, one of the newer points of interest on the island, is home to a drive-in movie theater, lots of abandoned vehicles, and a few neighboring buildings, homes, and structures within which you'll find some useful weapons, ammo, loot, and potentially, chests.

Smack in the middle of the drive-in's parking lot (at least during Season 4) is a crater created by a fallen comet. As a result, you'll find Hop Rocks in the area, which makes leaping around this region easier, and makes fighting adversaries a bit more interesting because everyone who consumes Hop Rocks becomes a harder target to hit.

This drive-in theater is loaded with old cars and trucks. Check the trunks and the backs of trucks for loot and chests.

Enter into the tractor trailer trucks to discover chests or other loot.

Crouch down when necessary, and use a vehicle for cover when you're engaged in a firefight against enemy soldiers.

The small building containing a snack shop might not look like much, but you'll likely find some goodies to grab on the ground or behind the counter. Don't forget to check the bathrooms.

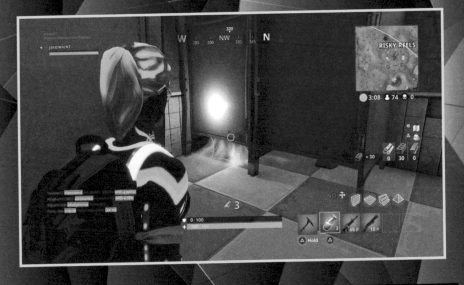

Always be on the lookout for that familiar glow emanating from a chest. There's one hidden in this bathroom stall.

This old house is located right near the drive-in theater. Explore it as you would any house.

Unless you land on the ceiling and smash your way through the roof, you'll need to build a ramp to reach the attic of this house, where you'll likely find a chest.

Salty Springs: Home Is Where Your Ammo Is

Out of all the points of interest on the island, the suburban neighbor-hood known as Salty Springs is probably the least interesting. Aside from a gas stations, what you'll find here are a handful of houses. Sure, you can explore the houses and find some loot, but don't expect to discover anything too amazing here. The more bizarre things to see and experience can be found at nearby Dusty Divot.

The homes may look different from the outside, but inside, each offers similar rooms, attics, and in some cases, basements to explore.

If you approach a home and see the front door (or back door) is already open (as seen on the previous page), or a wall has been smashed in, this is a good indicator someone has already explored the structure, so all the good loot has probably been taken. If you hear someone still inside, consider hiding out and waiting to attack them as they leave. If you're successful, you'll collect all of their loot once they're defeated.

This is one of the few homes in the area that contains a chest.

The gas station in Salty Springs typically doesn't offer too much (shown on the previous page). Don't waste too much time or energy trying to get inside safely. Move onto other more promising homes and structures.

This stone structure is definitely worth visiting, especially if you need to find and grab some weapons while you're visiting this area.

Always be on the lookout for Supply Drops. They typically land just outside of points of interest on the map. When you discover one landing nearby, approach with caution, and only if you need to expand your arsenal with some potentially powerful and rare weapons and loot.

Shifty Shafts: Explore a Maze of Mining Tunnels

This unique area (located at map coordinates D7) contains an old mining facility, some of which is above ground, but most of whose tunnels and places to explore are located underground.

The mining tunnels follow a maze-like layout, with blind turns everywhere. Located just outside the mining complex are two houses, as well as a demolished Battle Bus that has crash-landed on the island.

If you're approaching Shifty Shafts from the ground, look for this Battle Bus which crash-landed at the base of a nearby mountain. In addition to a chest, you'll find other loot in the area. Plus, as you make your way toward the mines, you can stock up on resources like wood and stone.

This view of Shifty Shafts from the top of a nearby mountain allows you to see many of the small structures above the ground, as well as the several entrances into the underground mine tunnels (shown on the previous page). Watch for enemy soldiers lurking around as you choose the best way to approach and enter this area.

From the outskirts of Shifty Shafts, and from the structures on the ground, you'll discover several ways to enter the underground tunnel area. Unfortunately, simply following the tracks does not always work.

Once inside the mine tunnels (shown on the previous page), crouch down and tiptoe, and keep your short-range to mid-range weapon drawn. Be ready to encounter enemies around each and every turn. You can't see what's happening around the bend, but if you listen carefully, you may hear enemy movement.

While exploring the mine shafts, look for crates you can stand on. Then, crouch down, aim your weapon, and wait for an enemy to approach. Being slightly higher than your enemy gives you a tactical advantage. Crouching down improves your aim. Instead of using a gun, tossing a grenade at an enemy, or setting a Trap, can also help you quickly defeat them.

Located outside, above the mine tunnels, there's a Vending Machine (shown on the previous page) that allows you to purchase weapons, if you have enough resources. Luckily, this area is chock-full of places to collect wood, stone, and metal, so chances are, you can collect what you need in the immediate area in order to make some useful purchases.

Take a short walk outside of Shifty Shafts, and you'll discover these two multi-level homes. Explore them just as you would any other homes. There are some chests to be found here, as well as other goodies.

Inside the homes you'll discover items lying on the ground. Don't forget to search behind furniture and staircases, look for hidden rooms, and make your way to the basement and/or attic, when applicable.

Snobby Shores: Where the Rich Come to Live and Supervillains Come to Hide

Located at map coordinates A5, Snobby Shores includes a lovely collection of waterfront mansions, most surrounded by security walls and guard posts. Be on the lookout for a Vending Machine located near one of the small stone buildings (close to one of the homes).

Surrounding Snobby Shores are two mountains. One has another home on it, but the other (located at map coordinates B4.5) has a secret base actually located inside the mountain itself. Because this point of interest is located close to the edge of the island, you typically won't have too much time to spend here before the deadly storm closes in and makes the region uninhabitable.

If Snobby Shores is your first stop after leaving the Battle Bus, you'll get a wonderful view of the waterfront homes in this upscale, suburban community as you're landing. Once you're on the ground, follow the paved paths to travel between the homes, or simply jump over or smash through the security fences in between each property.

Each multi-level home is loaded with weapons, ammo, and loot, along with at least one or two chests. As always, you'll typically find the best stuff in the attics or basements of each home. If there are a lot of adversaries in the area at the same time as you, each house also offers plenty of good hiding places from which you can launch surprise attacks, or just keep to yourself until the coast is clear.

Explore each room of the homes, and you'll often find random weapon and ammo lying on the ground.

Check the shelves for ammo boxes. Here, two ammo boxes can be found in the same room.

Outside many of the homes are these small stone buildings. Some were used for storage, and others were security stations. Be sure to open each door and look for loot inside.

efore entering a house, listen for nearby adversaries and peek inside
he windows. If you spot an enemy, shoot them through the window.

om the house on the nearby hill (map coordinates B6), you can see
he neighborhood below. Stand on the roof of this home and smash
hrough the ceiling to reach the attic.

The attic of the home on the hill contains a chest.

Grab what's inside this room, and then prepare to shoot at enemies as they climb the nearby stairs and literally walk into your weapon's line of fire.

If you don't land on the mountain that contains the supervillain hideout (map coordinates C5.5), you'll need to build a ramp to reach the top of the mountain.

At the top of the mountain is this small hut. There are no roads up here, so why is there a garage? Smash open the door, and you'll discover a shaft that leads downward. Welcome to the hideout!

Inside this hideout (located inside the mountain) is a giant missile. Why it's here may be revealed in the future, during Season 5. You can't smash it or destroy it, but you can explore all around it. Throughout this complex are numerous rooms that contain weapons, ammo, loot, and chests.

There are several chests to be found and opened within this hideout. This one is located within the empty swimming pool.

Another chest can be found in the bedroom.

This could be the control room for the giant missile. It's abandoned, however, so aside from finding random weapons, ammo, and loot on the ground, there's currently not much to do here but look around. This will likely change in the future.

Tilted Towers: Get a Taste of City Life on the Island

On the island, Tilted Towers is the closest thing you'll find to a major city. Sure, it has tall buildings, a clock tower, and a wide range of other structures to explore, but what it lacks are residents and traffic. Instead, you'll find heavily-armed enemy soldiers ready to shoot at anyone or anything that moves, as well as plenty of abandoned cars and trucks.

Try to avoid staying on ground level or out in the open for too long, especially when exploring the streets, because there are plenty of places overhead for snipers to be hiding. You'll find Tilted Towers near the center of the island, at map coordinates D5.5.

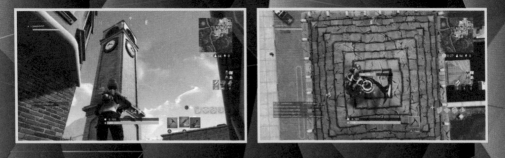

The clock tower is the tallest structure in the city.

Be the first person to land on the clock tower's roof and smash your way downward for a pleasant surprise.

As you smash your way down, you'll discover several levels in the clock tower, and most contain at least one chest, so by the time you make your way down to ground level, you'll have the opportunity to open at least three or four chests and collect the loot that's within them. Jackpot! Here, there are two chests next to each other, along with an ammo box.

You can always collect resources and then build a giant ramp to reach the top of the tower, but if you're not the first one there, it's kind of pointless since the loot will be gone. You'll find very few trees within

Tilted Towers, but there's plenty of metal and stone to be collected from the buildings and vehicles.

Knowing that enemy soldiers are going to be landing on the top of the clock tower, if you land on a nearby building and quickly collect a long-range weapon or sniper rifle, shooting at soldiers as they land on the tower can provide some easy victories. If you're the one landing on the tower, stay low and move quickly for cover into the tower itself.

Each building in Tilted Towers has multiple floors, which provides more places to explore.

The problem with Tilted Tower is that it tends to be a very popular landing destination. Once you land (and you're unarmed), if you don't move quickly and take cover, you will get shot within seconds. This is seen on the previous page.

Snipers are your worst enemies in Tilted Towers, but as a sniper, you'll have the opportunity to shoot at plenty of enemy targets. Notice the chest glowing in the far window. Wait until a soldier attempts to open the chest, and then take a few shots for an easy victory.

As you're about to land (as seen in the previous page), if you notice one or more other soldiers attempting to land on the same roof as you, choose a different landing destination, unless you're sure you will be the first person to grab a weapon. Otherwise, you'll be toast.

Look for hidden rooms, attics, and basements, because this is typically where you'll find the best loot. Expect to find enemies everywhere, so proceed with caution, with a weapon drawn, when entering any building or room. Weapons, ammo, and loot will be found out in the open, on the ground, in many rooms in buildings.

As you can see on the previous page, you will occasionally discover loo͗ outside, on ground level, as you explore Tilted Towers. It's very risky tᴏ be out in the open, however. Be ready to build protective walls arounᴅ yourself, and make sure you have at least 50 percent shields befor̥e placing yourself in a location where you're extremely exposed.

Remember to use the best weapon for the task at hand. A machine guᴿ worked well to take out this enemy soldier at close range. Be to build ᴀ protective barrier when you're out in the open and need to collect loot

Tomato Town: There's No Time to Enjoy the Food

Perhaps the reason this point of interest got its name was because thᴇ largest building here is a pizza restaurant. There's also a taco restauraᴎ and a gas station, along with a few houses within a short walk or jog You'll also discover bridges and tunnels outside Tomato Town that takᴇ you toward neighboring locations. You'll find Tomato Town at coordi-

Check out both levels of this pizza restaurant. An assortment of random weapons, ammo, and loot can be found here.

Most of what you'll find within the pizza restaurant is out in the open, lying on the floor and waiting to be snatched up. Don't forget to check behind counters and around the tables, however.

The gas station in Tomato Town and the taco restaurant, are both worth exploring, but you probably won't find too much loot or valuable goods here.

Located a short walk from the pizza restaurant you'll find a few remote houses. It's within these structures that you're more apt to find chests, as well as other useful weapons, ammo, and loot.

This house has a basement and an outside cellar door. Smash it open and go downstairs, where you'll discover several rooms, and at least one chest. Search the rest of this home, just as you would any other.

Perhaps the most interesting thing about this area is the tunnel that leads into or out of it.

About halfway through this tunnel, you'll discover this doorway off to the side.

Open the door and climb up the stairs. Alone the way, you'll discover some useful items to grab.

This is a bridge that's located about a one-minute jog outside of Tomato Town. Look for useful loot nearby.

Wailing Woods: A Dense Forest with a Maze

Located around map coordinates I3 is a large forest area. While this is a great place to stock up on wood, there's not much do or see here unless you traverse into the center of the region. Here, you'll find a hedge maze and a few wooded structures. It'll take some exploring (hopefully without getting lost), but there's a ton of great stuff to be found and collected here, including many chests.

As you approach Wailing Woods from the Battle Bus, all you'll see is trees, trees, and more trees—unless you make your way to the center of this region where there's a clearing.

While traveling through the dense woods, use your pickaxe to collect plenty of wood.

Near the center of Wailing Woods, you'll stumble upon the entrance to the hedge maze.

Use your pickaxe to smash your way through hedge walls, if necessary, to discover shortcuts through the maze. Listen carefully for the sound of chests and be on the lookout for their glow.

As you venture into this area, consider that enemy soldiers could be waiting for you around every turn.

Of course, you want to explore all of the wooden structures you come across as you explore the hedge maze.

everal of the wooden structures contain chests and other goodies.

you wind up getting lost in the hedge maze, try smashing your way
hrough the trees and bushes, or simply build a tall ramp to see where
ou are. You can expand the ramp into a bridge so you can quickly make
our way out.

SECTION 7
FORTNITE RESOURCES

Pro gamers around the world have created YouTube channels, online forums, and blogs focused exclusively on *Fortnite: Battle Royale*. Plus, you can watch pro players compete online and describe their best strategies or check out the coverage of *Fortnite: Battle Royale* published by leading gaming websites and magazines.

On YouTube (www.youtube.com) or Twitch.TV (www.twitch.tv/directory/game/Fortnite), in the Search field, enter the search phrase "Fortnite: Battle Royale" to discover many game-related channels, live streams, and pre-recorded videos.

Be sure to check out these awesome online resources that will help you become a better *Fortnite: Battle Royale* player:

Website or YouTube Channel Name	Description	URL
Epic Games' *Fortnite* YouTube Channel	The official *Fortnite* YouTube channel.	www.youtube.com/user/epicfortnite
Epic Games' official *Fortnite* website	Learn all about *Fortnite: Battle Royale*, as well as the paid editions of *Fortnite*.	www.Fortnite.com
Epic Games' official Twitter feed for *Fortnite*	The official *Fortnite* Twitter feed.	https://twitter.com/fortnitegame (@fortnitegame)
Fandom's *Fortnite* Wiki	Discover the latest news and strategies related to *Fortnite*.	http://fortnite.wikia.com/wiki/Fortnite_Wiki
FBR Insider	The *Fortnite: Battle Royale* Insider website offers game-related news, tips, and strategy videos.	www.fortniteinsider.com

(Continued on next page)

Game Informer Magazine's *Fortnite* Coverage	Discover articles, reviews, and news about *Fortnite* published by *Game Informer* magazine.	www.gameinformer.com/search/searchresults.aspx?q=Fortnite
IGN Entertainment's *Fortnite* Coverage	Check out all IGN's past and current coverage of *Fortnite*.	www.ign.com/wikis/fortnite
Jason R. Rich's Website and Social Media Feeds	Share your *Fortnite* game play strategies with this book's author and learn about his other books.	www.JasonRich.com Twitter: @JasonRich7 Instagram: @JasonRich7
Microsoft's Xbox One *Fortnite* Website	Learn about and acquire *Fortnite: Battle Royale* if you're an Xbox One gamer.	www.microsoft.com/en-US/store/p/Fortnite-Battle-Royalee/BT5P2X999VH2
Nomxs	A YouTube and Twitch TV channel hosted by online personality Simon Britton (Nomxs). It features *Fortnite* game streams.	https://youtu.be/np-8cmsUZmc or www.twitch.tv/videos/259245155
Sony's PS4 *Fortnite* Website	Learn about and acquire *Fortnite* if you're a PS4 gamer.	www.playstation.com/en-us/games/fortnite-ps4
Turtle Beach Corp.	This is one of several companies that make awesome quality gaming headsets that work great with a PS4, Xbox One, PC, or Mac. Being able to hear crystal-clear sound, plus hold conversations with fellow gamers, is essential when playing *Fortnite*.	www.turtlebeach.com

Your *Fortnite* Adventure Continues . . .

Epic Games continues to update *Fortnite: Battle Royale* with sometimes dramatic alterations to the island map; by introducing challenging new game play modes; by revealing exciting new storylines and subplots; by adding powerful new weapons and innovative types of new loot; and by making available eye-catching ways to showcase your soldier's appearance (with outfits, back bling pickaxes, gliders, emotes, and other customizable elements).

This game continues to evolve, ensuring that it never becomes boring, predictable, or easy to master. Even if you do get really good playing in Solo mode, when you gather one or more friends to compete with you in the Duos or Squads game play modes (accessible from the Lobby), the challenges and unpredictability within the game expand even more.

So, whether you experience *Fortnite: Battle Royale* on your Internet-connected Windows PC, Mac, PS4, Xbox One, iPhone, iPad, or Android mobile device, you're about to experience truly epic game play!

Now that you've discovered tons of useful strategies to follow, what will make you a truly awesome gamer is a ton of practice!

Good luck, and more importantly, have fun!